I0814873

# CHEERLEADING

# CHEER CAREERS

By Anita Banks

SportsZone
An Imprint of Abdo Publishing
abdobooks.com

abdobooks.com



Printed in the United States of America, North Mankato, Minnesota
052024
092024

Cover Photo: Gregory Fisher/Icon Sportswire
Interior Photos: Steven King/Icon Sportswire, 4–5; iStockphoto, 7, 14–15; Yuri Arcurs/Alamy, 8–9; Anna Stills/Shutterstock Images, 10; Hero Images Inc./Alamy, 13; Cathyrose Melloan/Alamy, 17; Phelan M. Ebenhack/AP Images, 19; Jeff Haynes/Panini/AP Images, 20–21; Ed Ruvalcaba/IOS/AP Images, 22; Steven King/Icon Sportswire/Getty Images, 24–25; Julio Cortez/AP Images, 26; Bob Levey/Getty Images Sport/Getty Images, 28; Chuck Burton/AP Images, 29

Editor: Christa Kelly
Series Designer: Kate Liestman

**Library of Congress Control Number: 2023949389**

**Library of Congress Cataloging-in-Publication Data**

Names: Banks, Anita, author.
Title: Cheer careers / by Anita Banks
Description: Minneapolis, Minnesota: Abdo Publishing, 2025 | Series: Cheerleading | Includes online resources and index.
Identifiers: ISBN 9781098293482 (lib. bdg.) | ISBN 9798384912750 (ebook)
Subjects: LCSH: Cheerleading--Juvenile literature. | Professions--Juvenile literature. | Sports--Juvenile literature.
Classification: DDC 791.6--dc23

# TABLE OF CONTENTS

CHAPTER 1

# CAREERS IN CHEERLEADING

Cheerleaders shine under the stadium lights. They perform in front of energetic crowds, awe audiences with their amazing skills, and work with their teams to execute incredible routines. For many people, cheerleading is a way to stay active and make friends. For some, it turns into a career.

There are many different types of cheerleaders. Some cheerleaders train and compete with clubs. These clubs

It takes a lot of skill and practice to be a cheerleader.

QTR 4
BALL ON 41

are often part of big cheer organizations. Other cheerleaders are part of a school's cheerleading team. These teams cheer for their school's sports teams during big games. Still other cheerleaders cheer professionally. These cheerleaders perform during games for professional sports leagues.

Similarly, there are many different jobs in the world of cheerleading. Coaches train and encourage their teams. Judges evaluate cheerleaders at competitions.

## CHEER ORGANIZATIONS

Many cheerleaders are members of cheer organizations. These organizations promote cheerleading and host competitions. They also provide safety education and create rules for competitions.

There are more than 3 million cheerleaders in the United States.

Choreographers create exciting routines for teams to perform. Professional sports cheerleaders serve as ambassadors for their teams.

No matter the job, people in cheer careers bring their love of cheerleading to their professions. Many were once cheerleaders themselves. A cheerleading career is a great way for people to continue working with an activity they're passionate about. It also allows them to inspire the next generation of cheerleaders.

CHAPTER 2

# COACHES

Every cheerleading team needs a coach. Coaches have many responsibilities. One of their first duties is choosing their teams. Some teams accept anyone who wants to join. Others have tryouts. During tryouts, coaches decide which cheerleaders would be the best additions to their team.

Once the team is selected, coaches may assign cheerleaders different roles within the team. Common roles include

Being organized is one of the most important parts of coaching a cheer team.

Coaches are responsible for registering their teams for competitions.

flyers and bases. Coaches assign these roles based on a cheerleader's skill, size, and strength. Coaches might also name a cheer captain. Cheer captains are usually selected for their leadership qualities.

Coaches are responsible for planning and leading practices. During practices, coaches teach new skills. These skills include various cheers and chants, stunts, and routines. Coaches also teach cheerleaders the rules of the activity.

## HIGH SCHOOL AND COLLEGE COACHES

College coaches are often in charge of recruiting new cheerleaders. When a coach finds a cheerleader who would be a good fit for the team, the coach will invite them to join. The school may give the cheerleader a scholarship to encourage them to join the team.

High school and college cheerleading coaches are also responsible for supporting their athletes, both inside and outside of cheerleading. Most schools require student-athletes to maintain good grades. Coaches are often responsible for keeping track of their cheerleaders' academic progress. Some coaches hold study sessions so that squad members can help each other with schoolwork.

## BECOMING A CHEER COACH

Different schools and organizations have different requirements for their cheer coaches. Some schools require coaches to have a college degree in sports management or a related field. Many also require experience in cheerleading or coaching similar activities, such as dance.

Some schools and organizations require their coaches to have a certification in coaching principles. People can get this certification by taking a class about coaching cheerleading.

The class teaches coaches about sportsmanship, conduct, discipline, and motivation. These classes are offered by cheer organizations.

Once coaches have the necessary qualifications, they can start looking for jobs. Coaching cheerleading teams can be either a full-time position or a part-time position depending on the employer.

## SAFETY

Safety should be a coach's top priority. Most coaches must be certified in first aid and CPR.

## CHEER INSTRUCTORS

Like coaches, cheer instructors teach cheerleaders new skills. However, instead of coaching a team, they normally work with young cheerleaders at cheer camps or cheer clinics. Most are current or former cheerleaders. They may teach at several camps each year.

**Some advanced skills, such as stunts, should be learned only under the supervision of a coach or instructor.**

The American Red Cross is one organization that trains coaches in these skills. Coaches can also take a course to receive the USA Cheer Safety Certification. This course teaches safety guidelines that are specific to cheerleading.

Coaches must also work to ensure their cheerleaders are performing safely. Cheerleading can be dangerous. Coaches teach cheerleaders the proper techniques for performing stunts and skills. They may also teach cheerleaders about nutrition and fitness.

CHAPTER 3

# JUDGES

Competitions are exciting events. During cheerleading competitions, teams perform impressive routines. They compete against other cheerleading teams. Some international competitions, such as the Cheerleading Worlds, attract more than 500 teams.

Cheerleaders practice for months before performing. When competition day finally arrives, it's up to the judges to decide whose routine is best.

Some cheerleading competitions have up to 11 judges.

## JUDGING COMPETITIONS

Competitions use a point system for scoring. Points are awarded for every aspect of a routine. Judges award points for clear cheers, synchronized movements, and smooth transitions between skills.

Harder routines can earn teams more points. However, added difficulty can also lead to more mistakes. Stepping out of bounds or losing balance can lead to deductions. Judges also deduct points for safety violations, such as missing spotters during stunts.

### SCORE SHEETS

During competitions, judges keep score sheets to tally points and make notes about each team's performance. These score sheets are used to determine the winning teams.

Some cheerleading competitions have thousands of participants.

Most competitions have several judges. During some competitions, the judges will separately score each team. The scores are then combined. The team with the highest overall score wins. During other competitions, each judge evaluates different parts of each team's routine. Performance judges evaluate a team's movements and stunts. Safety judges make sure teams follow the rules. Another judge might be tasked with evaluating a team's tumbling. Some competitions also have a head judge. This judge takes the other judges' comments into consideration to determine each team's final score.

Judging can be challenging. Competitions can last up to eight hours. In addition, when teams are performing, the judges must stay focused on the routine the entire time. They can't look away even to write notes. But they do get to see dozens of amazing performances.

## BECOMING A JUDGE

Judges need to know a lot about cheerleading. Many are former cheerleaders or cheer coaches. Cheer organizations train them to evaluate style, performance, and skill levels. Some people learning to judge go to competitions and train under an experienced judge. This is called shadow judging.

Judging is usually a part-time job rather than a full-time career. However, it comes with amazing opportunities. Some judges travel across the country or even around the world to judge cheer competitions.

Many cheer competitions end with an award ceremony.

CHAPTER 4

# CHOREOGRAPHERS

Cheerleaders need routines. Sometimes they are created by coaches. Other times, cheerleaders choreograph their own performances. But many higher-level teams rely on choreographers to build exciting routines.

Choreographers connect stunts, tumbling skills, and jumps to create captivating routines. They make sure that each move transitions smoothly to the next, and they pair their routines

Routines should be completed two to three months before the first competition to give cheerleaders time to practice.

TITANS

Some choreographers charge up to $4,500 per routine.

with music to make them more lively and interesting. Music also helps the cheerleaders stay synchronized.

## CREATING AND TEACHING ROUTINES

Choreographers are experts at creating the perfect routine for every occasion. For example, a routine for a young, beginning team will have easier skills. A team performing at a game will have energetic dance moves to get the crowd excited. And a routine for a competition team will be carefully crafted to earn the team as many points as possible.

Many choreographers also teach the cheerleaders how to perform their routines. They often teach the whole routine in a single day. They begin with a demonstration. Then, to help the cheerleaders learn the moves, the choreographers typically break the routine into smaller parts. They teach the team each part before putting everything together. This is easier than learning the whole routine all at once.

## BECOMING A CHOREOGRAPHER

Most cheer choreographers have backgrounds in dance or cheer. They often work with cheer organizations. The organizations pay them to make routines for cheer teams, camps, and schools. Choreographers may also work for colleges and professional sports cheerleading teams.

Choreographers often have a degree in dance or a related field. Getting a degree can help choreographers learn about music theory, proper dance techniques, and the creation of routines. Choreographers can also get additional certifications from dance companies.

CHAPTER 5

# PROFESSIONAL SPORTS CHEERLEADERS

Professional sports cheerleaders cheer for the most popular sports teams in the world. Their bold routines energize audiences during games. They combine dance moves, tumbling skills, and stunts to awe crowds.

These cheerleaders are among the most talented cheerleaders in their field. They usually have high school and college cheerleading experience or experience in dance or gymnastics.

**The average National Football League cheerleader makes about $22,500 per year.**

CHEERLEADERS
49

Teams sometimes offer classes to help cheerleading candidates prepare for auditions.

## AUDITIONS

Earning a spot on a professional cheerleading team is difficult. Only a few dozen teams have cheer squads. Earning a spot is highly competitive. Candidates need to audition. Some teams have hundreds of applicants and fewer than 40 open spots.

Auditions are held each year. They often take several weeks. The audition judges consider several criteria. One of the traits they're looking for is fitness. Cheerleading is hard work, so all cheerleaders need to be physically fit. Judges also look for skill. Cheerleaders need to be good at cheer and dance. Finally, judges evaluate the cheerleaders' attitudes. They want cheerleaders who are willing to work as part of a team.

## LIFE AS A PROFESSIONAL SPORTS CHEERLEADER

On game days, cheerleaders may have to work for eight to ten hours. They arrive at the stadium hours before the game starts. First, they warm up and practice their routines on the court or field. Then they go to their locker room to get their hair and makeup ready.

Before the game, cheerleaders might make appearances with the fans. They sometimes advertise merchandise. But their most important job starts when the game begins. Cheerleaders perform on the sidelines and cheer for their team. Their dances and cheers keep the crowd entertained.

Cheerleaders also have responsibilities outside of game days. Teams may have three to five practices each week. They might also make

**Some National Football League cheer teams host camps to inspire and train young cheerleaders.**

appearances for charity, such as visiting patients in hospitals or leading camps for young cheer teams.

Despite the long list of responsibilities, professional sports cheerleading is not a full-time job. Often, cheerleaders have other jobs or attend college. In addition, cheerleaders must practice and stay in shape during the offseason. That way they are ready for the next year's auditions.

Working in the world of cheerleading allows former cheerleaders to stay involved in an activity they love. It also allows cheerleaders to turn their passion into a lifelong career. Whether it involves working as a coach, a judge, a choreographer, or a professional cheerleader, a career in cheerleading offers fun and exciting opportunities.

**Cheerleading can help people make friends, gain confidence, and stay active.**

# GLOSSARY

**auditions**
Tryouts for a team.

**base**
The person at the bottom of a stunt who supports the flyer.

**certified**
Being officially recognized as knowing how to do something, often after completing a course.

**charity**
An organization that helps those in need.

**choreograph**
To plan a routine.

**clinic**
A class.

**CPR**
Cardiopulmonary resuscitation, an emergency procedure performed when a person's heart stops beating.

**evaluate**
To determine how good something is.

**flyer**
The person supported above the ground during a stunt.

**offseason**
The time of year when there are no games.

**routine**
A performance made up of individual stunts, tumbling moves, jumps, and dance moves.

**scholarship**
Money awarded to a student to pay for education expenses.

**spotter**
The person assigned to protect the flyer's head and neck during a stunt.

**squad**
A cheerleading team.

**stunt**
A skill in which a cheerleader is supported above the ground by one or more teammates.

**synchronized**
Performed at the same time as another person.

**technique**
The way a skill is performed.

**transition**
To move from one skill to another.

# MORE INFORMATION

## BOOKS

Banks, Anita. *Cheer Tryouts and Training*. Abdo, 2025.

Mooney, Carla. *Competitive Cheerleading*. Abdo, 2025.

Troupe, Thomas Kingsley. *Cheerleading*. Crabtree, 2022.

## ONLINE RESOURCES

To learn more about careers in cheerleading, please visit abdobooklinks.com or scan this QR code. These links are routinely monitored and updated to provide the most current information available.

# INDEX



## ABOUT THE AUTHOR

Anita Banks enjoys writing for children. She also enjoys reading, hiking, and traveling. Once upon a time, she was a cheerleader.